Running Your Church

A STRAIGHTFORWARD LOOK AT THE WORK OF CHURCH ADMINISTRATION

By

Sam Hunter

Copyright 2019

TABLE OF CONTENTS

ASSUMPTIONS ABOUT CHURCH

This is a straightforward book about the nuts and bolts of church administration. In plain language that means the day to day, month to month, and year to year operation of a local congregation organized in a specific place with a specific group of people who claim this as their church. The pastor is the public leader and face of a congregation, but there is much more that goes on behind the scenes that is sometimes overlooked and should be "top of mind" in the leadership of a church.

This isn't a book about theology or about denominational style or polity. The assumption is that you already have a concept of God, how you relate to him, and an idea of the mission you are to accomplish. What this book is about is how a local church really functions and how you can participate in the life and leadership of a church with a grasp of some key issues and how they might be addressed. Some churches have the feel that if you don't know something about how things work in the organization it is o.k. because only a select group of people need to know. Other churches spend time in classes and seminars teaching the tasks of ushering, or operating the kitchen appliances, or counting the offering without looking at the whole picture and how all of these tasks and activities fit together. So my perspective is to look at the big picture as well as the details and come up with a functioning integrated perspective.

The average church in the USA has fewer than 100 regular participants and yet there is something of value here for small congregations as well as large ones. The issues of church operation transcend size and the need for clear thinking is vital to all congregations. If your church has an administrator, a business manager, or an executive pastor then this book should be an aid to that person and to all of those that work alongside of them.

Finally, what is shared in this book is based on a lifetime of church attendance, participation, and professional work. I didn't aspire to a career in church administration, but through many circumstances I did spend 26 years in a career in church administration. Along the way I was part of churches of over 1,000 attenders and also part of churches in the 150 to 300 range. Academically I finished a B.A. in biology, an MBA, and a PhD in leadership. Over the years I've developed a deep appreciation of pastors and church staffs as well as the core leaders of every congregation. To all of my colleagues and acquaintances I offer God's blessing and good will.

WE HAVE A PASTOR

Every congregation needs a pastor. That person might be just at the beginning stages of being a pastor, they might be bivocational and have to work another job, they might have a Bible College or Seminary degree, or they might be moving to the end of a long career of effective pastoral ministry. Regardless of training and experience a pastor has an abiding sense of calling to be God's shepherd for a group of people and to represent God to them through all of the ups and downs of life.

Pastor's core orientation is people! This results in the consideration of things and systems being much lower on the list of priorities. Practically speaking, if you have a heart attack a pastor will do amazing things to see you and share God's hope and healing with you. But if the wall thermostat is broken a pastor may look dazed about why the building seems cold and wonder what is going on. A pastor will gladly accept an invitation for pie and ice cream, but forget to turn out the lights and lock up the church building. Church leaders and boards of directors want to hire a pastor that preaches great sermons, is the life of the party, understands the details of the annual budget, and can repair anything in the building. In the real world a pastor that preaches reasonably well and genuinely cares for the people in the congregation is the optimum. Financial expertise and the title of "Mr. Fixit" may not be the top items in a pastor's tool box.

Churches would be better served with the understanding that the pastor should be spending time preparing sermons and showing up at the parishioner's kid's ball games and band concerts and mixing with the leaders of the community at the local coffee shops. Mowing the church recreation field and expecting the pastor to repair the sheetrock wall that the teens bashed in is generally not a good use of the pastor's time and talents. If a congregation hired a pastor to be the caretaker for the building and grounds it is likely that the spiritual life of the church will suffer and may wither away. Most pastors I've known and worked with will gladly show up to help on a work day or spring clean up, but it is because of a desire to be with folks and not to get into a contest of how many pickup loads of leaves can be taken to the dump in the next 3 hours.

So the takeaway of this section is – spend some time thinking through what you expect a pastor to do and be. If the pastor is really hired to be the janitor then you just might have a very clean and very empty church.

OUR LAY PEOPLE WILL TAKE CARE OF EVERYTHING

In some churches things are organized by a faithful core group of leaders that are in charge. Sometimes the same folks have been in charge for 50 years and don't remember the church functioning in any other way. Pastors will come and pastors will go but this group is committed to making sure things are under control. Sounds like a great group to join and many an interviewing pastor has been lured to lead this type of congregation because of the appearance that everything related to the ongoing operation of the church would be taken care of by a committed core of lay people. The pastor would be free to preach and shepherd the wonderful people of the church.

This view of operating a church is problematic for several reasons. The first one is that committed lay people have a robust and busy life outside of the confines of their church. They have jobs and social commitments and times of being out of town and unavailable. Their attention to church is strongest on Sunday mornings and the occasions of a board meeting or small group. The majority of the time attention is focused in many other directions of work, family schedules, and a host of events. A common characteristic is for lay leaders to over promise and under deliver on projects and programs. In meetings with the pastor present, the core lay leadership will say, "We'll check on getting a new lawn mower this week." But months later a new lawn mower has not been acquired to keep the church front lawn looking nice. Perhaps the cordless microphone isn't working on Sunday mornings and the statement is made, "I'll contact a vendor and get a microphone this week." But by the next Sunday and the Sunday after that the Pastor is expected to preach with an older ineffective microphone or no microphone at all.

The second problem with this view of church operation is a struggle for control. This is often subtle but very real. The pastor is usually the loser in this arrangement because the lay leaders do not want infringement on an area of their control. For example the pastor may offer to initiate change in something like the church logo or web page and suddenly run into a huge objection from the core leadership. A pastor and the lay leadership may get embroiled in a lengthy and emotional exchange. Rather than join the effort in a collaborative way the issue is framed as an incursion into territory reserved for the lay leaders. A small number of these episodes will soon result in very few new ideas coming forward and a strong resolve on both sides to allow things to be "the way we've always done it." One characteristic of this is a pattern of board meetings where one or more lay leaders may make it their duty to "kick the beehive" to keep everybody and everything under control. The overall flavor of interactions among leaders becomes antagonistic and leads to a sense of "being stuck" with few decisions being made.

A third problem with this paradigm is the stagnation of leadership growth and a lack of openness to new lay leaders in the congregation. Leaders with a choke hold on the operation of the church and a resistance to new ideas and new people will do a great disservice to the mission and effectiveness of the church. In one congregation where I served on the board of directors it was soon clear to me that a small group of long time leaders had developed a style of "it's us against the world." They could not see that they were blocking the growth and forward progress of their pastor, and any new folks in the congregation that might be qualified and willing to join the team of leaders.

WHAT IS INCLUDED IN THE ROLE OF CHURCH ADMINISTRATOR?

For some readers this will be the most important part of the book because you've always wondered what those people do. Pastors, church boards, and human resources professionals can make this as simple or as complicated as they choose. I tend to like simplicity, so I'll offer my preferred description and then deal with some other options.

In general terms a church administrator facilitates the effective operation of a church so that the mission is accomplished by collaboration with the pastor, leaders and congregation in an encouraging way. So now to the specifics as determined by two questions. What has the congregation decided to do? What needs to be done to carry out what has been decided? So for a typical church functioning in a specific place this might describe the administrator's role in broad terms.

- Build and maintain a positive and collaborative relationship with the pastor, staff, and lay leaders of the church.

- Manage the facilities – building and property.

- Develop and manage a system of communication with the congregation and with the community.

- Oversee the financial operations of the church. This would include the development of an annual budget and efficient receipt and payment of moneys given to the church.

- Work with volunteers in the various programs of the church in a way that provides the tools and resources for them to succeed.

- Interact with the community of organizations, businesses, vendors, and residents around the church in ways that reflect the mission of the church and build positive and mutually beneficial relationships.

It is possible to add 5 to 10 specific sub points under each of the above, but that is something to do with care because more complexity does not necessarily translate to better work. Church administrators work in a dynamic environment with changing seasons, changing programs, and changing people.

So let's illustrate how the above items work in practice. In the start of a job as church administrator there is a pastor (generally, unless there is an interim), a secretary or administrative assistant, a janitor/grounds keeper, and then a group of ministry staff that might include: an associate pastor, a youth pastor, a children's pastor, a book keeper, a music and tech leader, and more possible positions depending on the size of the church. So as the new person it will be important to get the lay of the land in order to succeed.

BUILDING RELATIONSHIPS

Perhaps the pastor is an old friend, or a person you have known for a while. Now the relationship changes to one of working together on a day to day basis and will modify the interactions significantly. It will be important to get to know what is inside the head and heart of this key person you will be spending a lot of time with. Learning about the pastor's strengths and weaknesses will serve you well. Pastors live with the certainty that "Sunday is coming" and this usually drives their work week to be less intense at the beginning and more intense as the time for preaching arrives. Pastors are pretty human and not so divine if you spend a lot of time working with them. They have backgrounds and experiences that shape their identity and the way they make sense of life. You will be well served in engaging in positive inquiry about the background and life shaping experiences of your pastor. Some of the things you will want to know about: key attributes of a spiritual journey, family background and current dynamics, education and training, world view, and life mission. For example if the pastor you work with came from the south with a large extended family and now works in the northwest where individualism is the norm there will be some clashes of cultural points of view.

What was just stated about the pastor also applies to every member of your team of leaders in a local church. Each one is navigating life based on past experience and a bundle of values and expectations that you as the administrator didn't craft. It is in your best interest to seek understanding and forge a great working relationship with all of the staff in your church.

Here are some reasons why solid relationships matter. In the journey of church life there will be times of stress and misunderstanding that can be best weathered when there is a healthy relationship and a sense of support. It is a tremendous encouragement when you and your team feel valued and appreciated. Consider the idea of a box with many deposits of good will so that when stress and discord comes around there is enough positivity in the box to keep good working relationships intact.

THE FACILITIES

Most congregations either rent or own a place where they meet and carry out many aspects of their mission. I've been a part of downtown churches with nothing but the space of the building – no parking and no green space. More typically churches will have a parking lot and sometimes room for a volleyball court, a basketball court, a play area, or even acres of green fields for softball, soccer, and other activities. It might be helpful to include church owned vehicles under this category too. Some churches have a van and others will have a fleet of vans and buses. Regardless of size the facilities will require quite a bit of time and attention in the field of church administration. Let's take a look at the various facets of this challenging topic.

One of the most memorable moments in the life of a congregation is the point in time when they acquired property and constructed a building. If a history of the congregation is available this will certainly be a milestone that is recorded and documented. In a newer congregation people will remember this event and will recount the effort and the cost to get a place where the group could meet and do the things they want to do together as a church. Now for those of you with a strong perspective about the people being the church, you can relax but understand that a location and buildings are integral to the identity of a church. Just like a family inhabits a house, so the people of a church claim the place where they meet. If you strike up a conversation with someone and ask about their church affiliation it is likely you will get directions to the location of the property and then information about meeting times and programs.

As church administrator you will want to know the history of the property and buildings. This valuable information will lead to understanding of the story of the congregation and how they have been shaped by the location and types of facilities used by the church. For example I was a member of a church in the Midwest that had just moved to a new location and constructed a new and spacious building to serve 700 to 1,000 people. An important part of the story was that the congregation had been formed by a merger of two older established congregations: one relatively small with a congregation numbering under 100, the other of over 300 in a degrading inner city location. Thus the new location and new building held the promise of great things to come, but also represented the loss of historic and memorable properties with significant personal and financial investments. Some churches chafe under the reality of old and crumbling facilities when other congregations seem to soar along with new buildings and plenty of space. Whatever circumstance you may walk into as the church administrator get to know the history and ways the property and facilities have and are shaping the current life of the congregation.

A worthwhile approach is to look at a satellite image and identify characteristics of the church property and major items within a mile or two of the church. A variation of this is a series of drone photos of the church and surrounding environment. A rural church may be away from town on a farm road or highway frontage. One of the churches I served is within two blocks of a high school with 1300 students and close to the county fairgrounds. Another church that I served is landlocked on a city block with close parking adequate only for staff and a few guests. Using this approach you will see significant organizations nearby and patterns of pedestrian traffic and automobile traffic. This might provide a way to gauge the accessibility of the church facilities when small or large groups of people come for events. The regulars will know how to get into the building and where to park, but a guest may experience quite a challenge.

Another way to look at the church facilities is based on style of construction. Older buildings may have steps and small entry areas. This presents challenges to handicap access and transitions when congregants are coming and going with coats and boots. Small entry spaces and foyers don't foster much fellowship before entering the sanctuary or main meeting area. Is it easy to find the restrooms? And are the restrooms on the same floor as the large meeting room or sanctuary? Are the kitchen and fellowship hall on the same level as the sanctuary or is it necessary to go down a stairway or use an elevator? Some church buildings are easier to use and will facilitate the access and comfort of the congregation and guests. Traffic flow is important, but not always the first priority in the design of a building. The design of church facilities may make the work of the church administrator easier or very difficult. For example having a sanctuary that will seat 500 and a fellowship hall with seating for 100 may make it difficult to invite everyone to an all church potluck in the fellowship hall.

Maintenance practices of property and facilities make a very important statement about the congregation. I've walked into buildings that have not had anything fixed or upgraded for 40 years. Other congregations are forward looking and proactive about repairing, refurbishing, and remodeling facilities. On the exterior the presence of nicely trimmed plants and swept entries send an invitation to come in. When the outside is neglected or dirty, the expectations of long term attenders and guests are shaped long before they interact with anyone inside the building. Broken pavement with weeds or grass and shrubs long overdue for trimming send a huge message that works against all of the life saving and changing messages prepared for inside the facility.

Heating and air conditioning must be considered in the management of facilities. Some churches have heating systems that are difficult to manage and very inefficient. More than once I've heard church leaders say, "We only need the heat on Sunday mornings when we are here for church." Surely they are not considering the wear and tear on interior materials, musical instruments, and the general usability of the facility for funerals and other weekday events. Automated heating and cooling systems can shave many dollars off of utility bills while keeping the building within an acceptable range of usefulness. Many families relocate in the summer months and will begin the process of finding a church during this time. Imagine my surprise when a church leader remarked to me on a hot summer Sunday morning when there was no air conditioning, "We don't have enough hot summer Sundays to worry about. People will come back in the fall when things cool down a little bit." My observation is to remember that a church's building and property may tell your story before you get to do it through a sermon or over a cup of coffee.

The facilities dimension of church administration also includes several other important items. Casualty and property insurance are required. A well thought through fire protection and prevention plan is very important. Utility services include electricity, natural gas, water and sewer and garbage service. A host of other vendors will provide paper and janitorial products, coffee service items, and office products. Churches of today also need phone and internet service. And almost everyone will have a copy machine that will need servicing whether it is leased or owned. Other services might include snow removal, pest control, security system monitoring, and computer system maintenance.

One of the most important aspects of the dimension of church facilities is who has keys. Regulating and monitoring who can get in and who should not get in is tricky business. Some churches are very open handed with buildings and property. I've worked with groups that restricted the number of keys or fobs available and made people sign for them. In other cases keys were given to individuals using the building for an anniversary party or a piano recital with a reasonable expectation of responsibility for the security and tidiness of the building. It is a good idea to clarify the expectations of who, when, and why for the access and use of the building and grounds. One time I came to work on a summer morning and found three motorcycle riders camping in the church's outdoor gazebo. I enquired as to why they would camp at a church without prior permission. They responded that they considered church property relatively safe and that congregations were generous and would surely extend hospitality in this way to anyone traveling. Sometimes a sign with usage expectations is a good thing to post if campers, tractor trailers, and motor homes find their way onto church property for a night or a week.

COMMUNICATION

This is a very high profile activity for those that lead and work in churches. The importance of thorough and frequent communication can't be overstated. The methods and tone of communication may help with the transmission of the content or may make the content irrelevant. Gone are the days when congregational pastors and leaders assume that, "we mentioned it in the announcements last Sunday" is an adequate or effective way to communicate. So how does one navigate this strategic

aspect of congregational life when change seems to be constant?

A good place to start is to ask what kind of communication people

in the congregation prefer. A long time ago churches communicated with

announcements during services, paper bulletins, and a weekly or monthly

newsletter that was mailed. Sometimes these practices are still the rule

even though the congregation has moved to email, social media, and text

messaging in their day to day lives. It is worth a chuckle to watch a guest

enter a church and see the greeter try to stuff a bulletin into the hand of

person when they don't really want one. Some appropriate guiding

questions are in order. What should the people in the congregation know

about the mission and values of the church? How should people find out

about the schedule and programs of the church? What are good ways to

share spiritual stories and significant events with everyone? The answers

to these questions will require thoughtfulness and continuing effort. A

blend of all of the communication options might be the best approach.

Congregations of today are expected to have a digital presence. This will include at least a Facebook page, but more often involve a web page, social media accounts, and location information accurately appearing in a web search. The web page is probably the first place a person will look for information about a church. With that in mind the web site should tell the story of the church, the staff, and the programs. Making it difficult for people to find information will lessen the opportunity to meet them face to face. Many people use their phone to browse the internet so it is important to have the web site configured for both computers and phones. All of this requires a commitment to keep the information up to date. If the first thing to come up is an announcement about a Christmas program and it is now March you have a problem. There are many options in mixing and matching social media, but the question remains about which of the platforms your congregation uses.

Another issue in the communication arena is frequency. Many organizations assume that more is better. Some retailers try to send me information every day, but the effect is often not what they desire. If over communication happens with all of the tools available today, folks may not even bother if there is no perception of relevance. One suggestion is to communicate regularly, but make sure the content is meaningful to the recipients. A good question might be, "Would I be interested enough to engage in the message sent to me?" Social media is demonstrating the value of photos and videos loaded with meaning. Some platforms like Constant Contact enable you to see if people are opening and reading what you are sharing.

Paper and mail have value! Communication in this way needs to connect with people at the right time and in the right way. Women are the ones checking and reading mail. Men – not so much. But guess what – women are often the decision makers when it comes to scheduling and participation. It is helpful to realize that if you mail something late in the week and it arrives on Saturday, it may be buried or discarded because people want to take a break on the weekend. One theory of communication holds that it takes communicating a message 10 times before people will acknowledge and act on the information. So one post card may not work, but a repeated effort over a period of a few weeks might bring some great results. Feel free to test the effectiveness of paper based communication. How about offering a coffee coupon on the edge of the bulletin just to see if anyone notices?

Finally, a word about the tone of communication. Strive for a positive and hopeful tone in the many ways you communicate. I often remind pastors and church leaders that church participation and affiliation is voluntary. The journey through life is challenging enough without adding negative messages from my spiritual home, my church. Focus on the successes in loving and serving each other and reaching out to the community. Thank people for giving of time and money. Celebrate the achievements of congregants in school, in work, and in the community. Many church people have taken on large and difficult projects in the community and then find their church is not aware of their work or take an opposing stance without trying to understand the task and the issues. Living with an intentional connection between church life and the rest of life generates energy and hope. Experiencing little support and a big dose of criticism leads to discouragement and spiritual stagnation and eventual departure from the group. So take the issue of communication seriously!

FINANCES

Money is not the root of all evil! But poor practices at church with all matters financial may soon lead to sudden ruin. I've sometimes said that bigger offerings would surely solve some of the ongoing problems at church. In light of increasing costs of operations for churches a few more dollars of giving really does make a difference. The real issue here is the concept of stewardship. Setting up a good foundation for stewardship is very important. Here are a few questions to ask. Who are the owners of the church, including property, buildings, and equipment? What mission is being carried out with the resources of the church? Are the resources available to the congregation primarily for their internal use? Is the package of money, buildings, property, and equipment considered a tool for accomplishing a life changing mission? Is the pastor, the board of directors, or the denomination considered the ultimate controller of finances and other resources? With our best thinking in place let's dive into this topic in more detail.

Fundamental to working with the resources of a church is the concept of trust. Putting it simply trust is marked by honesty and reliability. My experience has been that money and resources are more likely to flow to organizations demonstrating stewardship and trust. So a commitment to trustworthiness should be made by the pastor, the church staff, and the key leaders. Systems should be in place for the handling of incoming funds through offerings and gifts and the expenditure of funds in the operation of the church. Specifically the church should develop and approve an annual budget and have a specific plan to handle incoming funds and expenditures. Most churches have rules about having at least 2 people present to handle money. Many computer systems are available to facilitate bookkeeping, accounting, and the proper receipting of contributions. Choose and pick tools for the financial operation of the church that are straightforward and easy to use. It is discouraging for a secretary, bookkeeper, or volunteer to use a financial system that is cumbersome and time wasting. Separating handling of money from expending money is a key safeguard. It is best if a team of people take the financial responsibility of the church so that the reputations of staff and volunteers are protected. Monthly reports to the board of directors should be the norm. Annual reviews by a professional firm or a team of church leaders not involved in the financial affairs should be scheduled and the results shared with the congregation.

A healthy church needs an annual budget. It is an agreed upon road map of financial direction and goals for a year. Developing a budget that considers how much money comes in and how much money goes out can be done in many ways. One quick way – agree to throw the offering in the air and whatever comes down can be used as needed – just kidding! Congregational culture sets the approach to budgeting. On one end of the spectrum are churches that believe in journeying strictly by faith and they will not develop an income number because this is viewed as presuming on God's will. At the other end of the spectrum are churches with annual

pledge campaigns. The total of all of the annual giving pledges

determines the income number and hence what can be expended. The

truth is income and expenditure forecasting is in between these ends of

the budgeting practices spectrum. Here are some relevant questions for

the budget development process.

- What is God calling the congregation to do? Responses from the
  Pastor and key leaders to this question will help with the overall
  direction. For example if there is a compelling vision to reach
  children and families, funds would be needed to add staff and
  resources. If a group of people has asked that the restrooms be
  fixed and updated this will require funding for a project. Perhaps
  a group has a sense of calling to start a new church or a satellite
  location and needs start up funding. The spiritual calling of
  leaders should definitely be considered in budgeting.
- What is happening to the congregation? Is it growing? Stable?
  Declining?

- What is happening in the community where the church is embedded? Is there a recession or a boom? Are people moving into the area or leaving? Is there a baby boom? Are retirees moving to the area?

- What are other churches in our area experiencing? Are they growing? Has something negative affected all churches? Is something positive going on?

Here are some practical suggestions for the budgeting process. Look at the income and expense records for the last 5 years. Is income increasing, stable, or decreasing? Prioritize the key expenses so you have an idea where there may be some flexibility. Pastor and staff compensation and benefits may take up to half of the entire budget. If the church has a large property and facility the costs may take a larger slice of the budget. Put your thinking cap on with the leaders of the church and ask, "How can folks in the congregation be encouraged to give to support the mission of the church?" "Are there creative ways to reduce spending or reallocate spending?" Use of a computer software program can make the budgeting process straight forward, but you can outline it on the back of a napkin. Set up categories of income: tithes and offerings, bequests, gifts, other. Set up categories of expenses with as much detail as necessary: Salaries and benefits, mortgage, utilities, programs, missions, and other. The budget you develop may require 2 or 3 meetings to develop. It is also wise to have an understanding that the budget can be changed with the approval of the church board during the budget year. Things can change: income may drop or a leading program may end. Work with the leadership team on any adjustments that are made.

If your church is alive and breathing, money will be handled. The key question is where, when, and by whom? Cash and checks that are collected in the offering have to be put somewhere, counted, and then taken to a bank. Even in a very small church it is not a good idea for the pastor to handle money. Pastors that handle money are vulnerable and subject to accusation for even the appearance of impropriety. So a better approach is to have a team of at least 3 people handle money. They count it; record it with documents showing their signature, and take deposits to the bank. If another church member or staff member take deposits to the bank, make sure that the cash and checks are in a sealed bag or envelope that only the bank can open. Some readers may believe that church donations are all online or via debit card or debit card. It is true that online and card donations are becoming more common, but most churches still have cash and checks coming in. A photocopier provides a wonderful way to record checks and accurately get the information from them for acknowledgement of giving by the donor. Many forms have already been developed for use in counting money and checks, so find and use forms that make sense for your particular church.

Many churches accumulate cash and checks from the offering and hold it in a safe until it is counted. Two people collect and place the money into the safe so that they are both protected. At a later time two people should collect the offering when it is to be counted. The principle is not about the effort of the people involved, but about answering the question, "Was the money handled in a trustworthy way?" Usually a secretary or bookkeeper enters into a computer program the particulars of income in the form of cash, checks, or online giving. Again there should be a way to check for accuracy and reliability. The administrator should have the ability to check the entries. Certainly the church board will be getting reports of income and expenses each month and should be knowledgeable to ask good questions and spot check the process. The expected recommendation of reviewers and auditors will be the separation of tasks and cross checking of deposits and expenditures.

What tools should a church use in the handling of money? Usually offering plates or offering bags are used during services, but some groups use a deposit box in the foyer or in the sanctuary. A reasonably sturdy drop safe in a locked room is a good tool for holding money on site. During the counting process recording forms for cash and checks and a copy machine for records of checks should be available. Sealable or lockable deposit bags should be available for deposits being taken to the bank.

This is a good time to talk about banking relationships. A church will need a banking partner and many banks take a favorable view of churches and will go the extra mile to serve them. So find a bank that is compatible with your church and establish a good working relationship with the staff and management. In my experience a healthy banking relationship can save you some money and will help if there is an issue with a deposit or a transaction. For example on one occasion our bank called late in the week to say that we were overdrawn in our main checking account. I was puzzled, but wondered why that would be the case when there was a substantial offering on the previous Sunday. I asked about the most recent deposit and found that a member of the financial team had put the sealed bank deposit bags in his car, but due to a family event had forgotten to take the deposit bags to the bank. Hence, while our records at church showed funds had been counted and deposited, the call from our friendly banker helped us track down the missing deposit.

It is important to understand the relationship with banks and other financial institutions and their role in the life of your church. At some point your church will likely have a mortgage related to the acquisition of property, the construction of a building, or the remodel of facilities already being used. The key question is how do we accomplish what needs to be done as good stewards and as people of goodwill in our community? Most financial institutions have a process and a decision making framework for granting loans and mortgages. Many of these organizations have decided that churches are a poor risk and have chosen to stay away from churches because of potential ill will if financial affairs go the wrong way and the bank is forced to foreclose on a property or other assets. However, some financial institutions have decided to focus a part of their business on churches because it is within their mission and they have a genuine interest in helping churches and other nonprofit organizations. So the task of establishing and maintaining a good relationship with a bank or credit union is very important. At one time I served on a church board when the church had construction bonds with an interest rate of 22% and church leadership knew this would not be sustainable. But there was uncertainty in developing a plan to reduce this staggering debt. After some deliberation one board member offered to draft a letter outlining the church's need for a loan and to send it to 60 financial institutions in the metro area to see if there was interest in helping the church. Shortly after the letters went out a nearby bank contacted the church and offered to learn more about the situation. It turned out that the chief executive of this local bank grew up in a church and understood the workings of a church extremely well. He had influence over the approval of loans by the bank's lending committee. Soon a mortgage was in place that reduced the interest rate dramatically and allowed some financial breathing room for a growing congregation. Over the years I've found that it pays to look around for the best terms, a good working relationship, and a manageable plan for the congregation. If there is no chemistry with the financial institution and the mission of the church, you should look for a more compatible partner in this important aspect of church life.

Folks in your congregation are going to spend the money! The prudent church has a clear system of who can spend funds, how expenditures are approved, and how staff and volunteers can get reimbursed when they are carrying out the mission of the church. With this topic there is a continuum of practice: In some churches all expenditures must be approved by the board of directors in advance and at the other end of the spectrum individuals know that if they are acting within a program framework on behalf of the church they will be reimbursed. The question to answer here is what works? And a second question is what level of control is needed? In many churches the official position is that budgeted expenses are planned, but if a volunteer buys pizza for a teen event, it is considered a non-reimbursable expense. So it is important to have a conversation and understandings with the leadership about how things are paid for. One advantage of requiring prior approval is that spending funds can be absolutely controlled. The downside is that folks won't seize an opportunity when it could really make a difference.

Two ladies involved in the compassionate ministry of the church came by the church office one day. They had just discovered a family needing a washer and dryer. Laundry was stacking up, kids were out of clean clothes, but the family didn't have the money to get different appliances or even repairs. In my role as church administrator they included me in the deliberation about what to do for this family. One perspective was to wait until a regular committee meeting met in the coming month. The other perspective was to move forward with the acquisition and installation of a used washer and dryer and solve the problem. I asked how much urgency they felt about the situation and if they had enough money on hand to move forward. It was a short conversation and really dealt with the concept of being empowered to extend the love and grace of the church to a family that needed some help. I supported them in the question of, "Could we help?" while they worked on the question of, "Should we help?" Money and other resources are needed to accomplish the mission as a church. Do you have a system in place that fosters the accomplishment of the mission or a system that stops people from moving forward when they could express the love and compassion of the church body?

The pastor and church staff have an inside track on spending money. It is wise to create a clear understanding of who can spend money and for what purpose. Churches may grant an expense account to the pastor and other staff like youth pastors. My experience shows that pastors and associates are often big hearted, but terrible with record keeping and receipts. A good way to come along side them is to develop a workable system with them that makes it easy to show when and why expenditures were made and where they are in a monthly or annual budget. I've worked with church staff that could account for every penny. I've also worked with those who couldn't find receipts and could not remember a particular debit card expenditure. There is a balance of discipline and grace here, but if stewardship in handling money is viewed as a waste of time, there may be problems on the horizon in other areas of work and ministry. A lapse in accountability in this area can bring everyone in leadership down!

STAFFING AND COMPENSATION

The pastor, secretary, youth director, janitor and everyone else on the team want to be paid! The goal of local churches is to be fair with compensation. But how do you do this when there is some tension between paying the pastor and staff and taking care of local programs and having something left for global missions? Here are some key questions to consider that focus what to pay and how much the congregation can afford. The first question to answer is, "What is our total annual giving?" The second question is "What does it cost to live in our area?" The third question is "What staff does our church need to accomplish the mission we are called to do?"

If you are part of a new church or just beginning to think of starting a new church the question of annual income may not have an answer. Congregations that are in a home – under 30 people – may not be concerned about the amount of giving needed to support a small congregation. In a house church everyone is a volunteer and the hat is passed to help the host home with utilities and wear and tear. The group can decide to contribute to local or global causes in very spontaneous ways. This is a style of church life that requires little in terms of financial resources in an ongoing and systematic way. However if you are starting a church it is good to build a roadmap of financial requirements for the first few years. Most congregations are no longer start ups and they are old enough to grapple with questions of a paid pastor and the costs of a dedicated place to meet and hold events.

Paying a pastor and running facilities requires some minimal level of income. For example if the congregation has ten families and all of them are committed to a 10% tithe it is possible to have $100,000 in income. Thinking of an even split you could pay a pastor $50,000 per year and spend the other $50,000 on building costs. If the church were to grow and stay in the same facilities it is possible to have more funds available for pastor and staff, but building costs will increase over time.

The second important question is "What does it cost to live here?" A good way to approach an answer is to look at minimum wage jobs and then look at pay for professionals like school teachers, bank tellers, and medical staff. It is also o.k. to call some churches in the area and ask what their pay range is for pastors and staff. Church people often assume that compensation is a "black box topic" that is so spiritual that no one really knows. My advice is to put your best thinking cap on and remember that professional clergy and staff are not unaware of the cost of living and the pay it will take for them to make it successfully while working for the church. People with a strong sense of divine calling will consider working in your congregation if they feel you are treating them fairly. So do your homework and know how much you can spend for a pastor and staff. If you are part of a church with a completely volunteer pastor and completely volunteer led programs for children and youth it is likely you will get the time and energy left over after they have worked at another job. In a bivocational arrangement where the pastor works at another job and is paid part time by the church it is very possible the other job will claim that person's best time and attention. So if you can fund a full time pastor the congregation will benefit from a person singularly devoted to the spiritual well-being and nurture of the people. If a church has an administrator or executive pastor the decisions and operation of the church will be enhanced in ways that maximize the time and resources of the group. Be fair with your congregation and staff. Hire the folks you need and pay them fairly!

Answering the question of "What staff does our church need to accomplish the mission we are called to do?" is complicated for several reasons. Some pastors and congregations natively organize for a full complement of staff. In this case people have had prior experience and know what this looks like and how to navigate in this way. If a group of church leaders move to a new area to start a church they will bring prior experience and ideas with them. However if a congregation starts from nothing and moves forward there will be multiple forks in the road with accompanying decisions. Congregations have many things in common with small businesses. Operational characteristics based on size are one of the things that are similar. In the business world the often used word is "scalability." I am attending a church with a choir that sings every Sunday. The church is growing and the choir is growing as well. This might seem odd to some readers, but churches need to pay attention to what is happening in the current situation. So one Sunday I was sitting by the attendance taker for the choir and he remarked, "Wow we have a lot of people in choir now." So wondering if he was willing to think about this phenomenon I asked, "What would you do if the size of the choir doubled?" He just looked at me and didn't really respond. To be fair I knew that over the last decade the same choir had dwindled to the point where it seemed difficult to have a couple of people sing each part in a cohesive way. But a new pastor arrived and attendance and participation started to increase to the point that the choir was running out of space and running out of chairs. To not think of growth and its implications is really just another way to think of growth. Taking another viewpoint, if the youth group in a church has doubled in size and the volunteer team is stretched to the limit when will the leadership of the church move to bringing in a youth pastor? I have a friend whose dad was a pastor. It was his dad's mission to never pastor a church with more than 100 people. So if the pastor and leadership have a particular size in mind based on preference or experience, this may well dictate the issue of size and the number of people working at your church. As the size of a church increases so does the complexity. Some congregations have a culture comfortable with a larger organization and some do not. If you are in the administration of a church, it will serve you well to know the sentiment of the congregation relative to size in attendance, resources, and staffing.

RISK

If you are in church administration you have to deal with risk. Included here are several subtopics: insurance, security, and a proactive or reactive stance. One great question to prime your thinking is, "What are the chances ...?"

Insurance is a tool for managing risk in casualty, health, and challenges to the organization or its leaders. Casualty insurance deals with the possibility of loss or damage to property and facilities. Included in this would be fire, flooding, storm damage, or a law suit stemming from a fall or other injury. A good course of action is to find a capable insurance professional and work with them. Make sure they understand your church and the programs you conduct and why. My church started a summer day camp that ran for several weeks and was based in the church facility. The capable insurance professional working with us made an appointment to observe this new venture. He wanted to be certain the congregation had an appropriate level of liability protection for this venture. The underwriter of our annual policy was unfamiliar with this type of program and therefore our agent spent time explaining the intent and the operational details of the program to the underwriter. The result was a fair policy with coverage for this important program.

As the church administrator I was the one contacting our insurance carrier to report storm damage, or an injury on a teen outing, or a fender bender with the church van. In all of these cases it is easier to speak with someone on the insurance side that you have a relationship with instead of a claims manager with little or no familiarity with your church. Even in this age of computerization it really does make a difference if you can work with a person with whom you can build a relationship. For several years our insurance agent made it a practice to physically come by the church and meet with me and tour our property and buildings. In hindsight this commitment helped both of us accomplish our work as good stewards.

Health insurance is ever changing! In the 1980's and 1990's churches, districts/regional offices, and denominations provided health insurance for pastors and church staff members. At one point in the early 1990's I took a look at our church's health insurance costs for 3 full time staff and their families and realized the church would go broke with the 10% increases in premium costs each year. So we went shopping and had to tailor the insurance plans to make a safety net for our church staff. Over the years the challenges continued with rising costs and diminishing services. Currently our church provides each staff person a set stipend and allows them to find the health insurance and level of care they prefer. So a worthy guideline is to provide a safety net and as many add on benefits as the congregation can afford. In one season we had a young staff member with a major heart problem. This made the premiums for our small insured group sky rocket. It wasn't fair, but it was a reality we faced together.

Church work is considered high risk! News of sexual impropriety, child abuse, and church shootings moved the perception of church work to very high risk. In your commitment to the calling and mission of your church you will have to deal with this seemingly unfair operating environment. Efforts to be proactive with this topic will have great value for your church and community. The first step is to know your congregation and especially those in leadership positions. Failing to know the backgrounds and limitations of people in the congregation is not acceptable. For example for several years I worshipped with a transformed man with a drug filled felony record past. To deny his past was foolish and to place him in a role without regard for his past would have been unwise. On another occasion a man began attending and soon volunteered that he had a legal past that prevented him from any contact with children. He was not a threat, but needed help to honor these boundaries. So if you are the church administrator, make it a practice to learn about the people in the congregation. You have great tools available with background checks and screening procedures and these can be coupled with help from law enforcement. Pay attention to your inner voice and the observations of others you trust within the congregation. Make it a practice of looking out for each other and gate keeping for children and elderly.

One week I was doing a walkthrough of the church sanctuary early in the week. By the way - church administrators are encouraged to frequently walk around just to observe the state of things. As I walked along the back of the sanctuary I noticed something shiny in the back pew. On closer inspection the shiny objects were a handful of bullets! My mind just about exploded as I picked up the bullets. In recent years, school shootings and church shootings were more frequently reported in the news. In the middle of my shock I remembered that there was a gunsmith in the congregation. We had recent conversations about projects underway and restorations he was doing on valuable and historic guns. Then I realized this was the area where he typically sat during church services. So I made it a point to return the bullets to him and share my anxiety about finding bullets in a pew. He admitted some dismay about the loss of bullets he had in a pocket!

VOLUNTEERS

Church life is all voluntary! I've often reminded myself and my colleagues at church that people participate in church life because they want to. This fundamental reality in church administration is sometimes forgotten. The good people in the congregation are not working for you or the pastor for a paycheck. Taking time to think through the methodology of working with volunteers is critical. Two dimensions of working with volunteers stand out: one is value and the other is honor. Scripture has much to say about the treatment of individuals in the community of faith and I urge you to spend some time finding the relevant statements. My focus is on the strategy for successfully working with volunteers.

I've been in churches where the operating model is to fill all the positions of responsibility with warm bodies. Imagine how awkward it is to be assigned to teach a group of 5th grade boys when the leader has no prior experience with children's groups or with teaching. Or think of the discomfort of a person charged with maintaining a church vehicle when in their own life they don't know how to check the oil in a car they own. So a couple of questions are salient here, "What do you feel called to do in our church?" and "How has your background and experience prepared you to make a contribution of your time and talents in our church?"

One significant concept is that every person has value. Acknowledging the inherent value in volunteers increases the meaning of church involvement significantly. The contributions of volunteers within the congregation may cover a wide spectrum, but they are all important to the effectiveness of the church community. I had the pleasure of knowing a lady that was a really good cook. The topic of church gatherings would come up and she would volunteer to prepare main dishes for events. One of her mouth watering creations was "Chicken Chalupa." She was an experienced cook and knew how to feed a lot of people. She would remark to those planning events, "Don't ask me to turn on my stove for a handful of people. Call me when you want to feed a hundred or more." What a delight to know there are volunteers like this great cook! Folks in the church raved about her dishes and everyone was blessed by the contribution she made through her cooking.

I walked into a church choir room and was shocked to see how shabby it was. The walls were stained by water from a prior leak in the roof. Carpeting was worn and dated and the coat racks and shelves were junky. When I asked about the contrast of the choir room with a newly remodeled sanctuary I was told that there just weren't enough resources to remodel both. So I pondered the situation and waited until a good time to see if something could be done about the choir room. Within a few months the congregation temporarily moved out of the sanctuary for a major construction project. All of the services were conducted in the gym and the choir room was vacant for a few months. So the day came when I had the opportunity to speak to the chairman of the facilities committee about the sad state of the choir room. We took a tour of the choir room and discussed the peeling paint, broken lights, and worn carpeting. In a few days he let me know that he had a plan for updating and cleaning up the choir room. I didn't think much about the project for several months until the sanctuary was ready to be used again for regular services. It was a joy to enter a choir room with new paint, new lighting, new flooring, and a welcoming atmosphere. In conversations with fellow choir members we considered ways to say thank you for such a great improvement. Finally it was decided that an acceptable way to honor the work of our friend was with a homemade apple pie. The pie was joyfully received along with our thanks for such great work. Fixing the choir room was done behind the scenes and a public recognition wasn't valued. People in the congregation have significant contributions to make and the challenge is to make it easy for them to utilize their gifts and abilities while honoring them in appropriate and meaningful ways.

THE COMMUNITY OUTSIDE

Churches aren't islands unto themselves. They exist in particular locations and within communities and cultures that are unique. Often this aspect of building relationships with the organizations, businesses, vendors, and residents around a church isn't given enough attention.

My friend working next to me at the church was surprised by the negative view of our church that was held by the owner of the automotive shop where he took his car for repairs. It wasn't about the theology of the group or about the color of the building. He was displeased with a group of teens playing basketball at the church's outdoor court late on summer evenings. His house was across the street from the church and the sounds of a group playing made it difficult to sleep. He needed to be at work very early in the morning and felt the church people were not being considerate. My friend asked if he knew anyone from the church. The answer was a resounding no!

Church administrators are shapers and keepers of the interactions of the church in the community. The reputation of the church is developed through the ongoing interactions with the surrounding community. The pastor may preach some of the best sermons in town, but if the church doesn't pay bills on time or if the garbage truck driver often finds the access to the dumpster blocked the reputation of the church in the community will suffer. Some relevant questions might help. Do we know the people and organizations immediately around our location? What is the perception of the church in the community?

So what does this dimension of church life look like and how can it be improved? If you are working at a church or are somehow responsible for business relationships it will serve you well to get to know the regular suppliers and vendors of the church. In one week you could see the mail delivery person, the package delivery person, a cleaning supplies representative, the copier maintenance person, at least one homeless person, and others coming to inquire about using the building, or about church programs. In all of these encounters you represent the values of the church and embody the message preached on Sundays.

One day the cleaning and paper supplies account manager came by the church to drop off some items we ordered. I asked how things were going. His countenance dropped and he asked if I was serious in my question. Then he told me the company he worked for had been sold and the new owners doubled his territory, closed the closest distribution warehouse, and discontinued a delivery truck taking product to the accounts he was serving. This was all in the name of reducing cost and increasing profitability. He teared up and said, "I just don't know if I can continue to work this way. I am at my limit and my hours are so long I am not home much." I really didn't know what to say except to listen and offer that our church valued his work and service. Time went by and the day came when he joyfully reported that the company had a new owner. His smile had returned as he told me how the new owners met with him and asked what the company could do to support his work with a growing number of commercial accounts. "You know I was at my lowest point when we chatted. Thanks for listening when things didn't seem like they could get any worse." The message of your church will flow across the many relationships with vendors and other organizations in the community. This is such an important matter that you would do well to develop a strategy for this area of church administration.

CHURCH SECRETARY

Church secretaries will have a special place in heaven! Working with a group of clergy and professional ministry leaders is quite a challenge and is much different than similar work in business organizations. The secretary is often the first person the members and attenders will meet. The calls and walk-ins coming to the church will also likely encounter the secretary first. Let's take a look at the role and work of the secretary in relationship to the overall administration of the church.

Church secretaries or administrative assistants are key people in the overall operation of church. Over the years I've interacted with these people in large and small churches. Sometimes the position is part time with limited hours and responsibilities. In other situations a team of folks work together in this important role. Usually the church secretary is the person officially responsible for phone calls, mail, general email, records management, calendar management, scheduling, and supporting the work of the pastor and others working at the church. This position involves trust, confidentiality, and interpersonal skills. The secretary working at your church can make or break the entire effort of the organization. It is not a job for the faint at heart or for those with untested faith. The work involves working with people and organizations on a tight weekly schedule while navigating the ups and downs of life. Pastors are frequently semi depressed in the early days of the week and then push hard to get sermons, power point presentations, and meetings with colleagues and parishioners done by the end of the week.

Secretaries often work alone and need self motivation and self management to accomplish and balance the work coming to them. A steady flow of information comes in: email, regular mail, financial contributions, notices of births or deaths, requests for facility usage, prayer needs, and many requests to share messages with the congregation through the bulletin, newsletter, or online. Information comes along at the best and worst of times and often is confidential. A church secretary may also be the social planner for the staff in terms of birthdays, seasonal parties, or informal celebrations. The one common expectation is for the secretary to be there and know what is going on.

How does a church administrator or executive pastor work with a secretary? In the best scenario the administrator makes the life and work of the secretary better. Take a look at work load, life/work balance, and compensation. Being an advocate for the secretary of the church is a way to move toward the optimum outcome for the church and for the individual working as the secretary. Helping a church secretary succeed will make the administrator job more productive and will set the pastor, staff, congregation up for a positive and productive journey in accomplishing the mission of the church. Here are some examples.

Linda was working in a church of 700 with a pastor, an associate pastor, a youth pastor, and a children's ministry director. She was an energetic person with the ability to manage multiple projects, engage people, and get lots of work done. It was during this time I was serving as

a board member at the church and admired the work Linda did. But I

noticed Linda was frustrated with things in the office and wondered what

would improve the situation. It turned out that in this era of office

technology the church was beginning to invest in computer equipment,

but had not provided a printer with connections and capability to

complement word processing. When I asked what options had been

considered, Linda offered that she couldn't move forward because there

was no money for additional office equipment. This surprised me. So I

did some investigation on my own and purchased and donated a small

printer that could be used in the current work space. The printer

leveraged her work considerably and kept her from quitting over such a

small issue. Everyone benefitted from this small improvement! Neither

the board nor her colleagues seemed to be aware that this was a big deal.

In another case I was the administrator at a church when there

was a change in secretaries. The new person was taller than the

predecessor. So I asked the new hire to research office chairs and pick one out that would function in the work space. She looked very surprised to be given this option, but I offered that a comfortable chair would make work easier and less physically stressful. We agreed on a choice of chair and she was off to a more comfortable time at work every day. By the way, office chairs don't last forever. So it is important to think about the ergonomics of the church secretary's work environment. Desk space and lighting should be on the list of considerations too.

Technology is ever changing for church secretaries. In one church office the large desktop computer system began growling and then shutting down unexpectedly. The secretary mentioned the problem, but continued to patiently work with this system where the noise level was increasing and the reliability of document storage was getting worse every day. It was clearly time to do something, but who had the authority to acquire a new computer and then transfer all of the information and get it up and running? Approval was required from the chair of the technology committee on the church board. Agreement on price, vendor, and implementation plan needed to be in place to move forward. It

wasn't a quick fix, but working together we upgraded the computer.
Imagine the sheer joy of the secretary when the day came when a new
smaller, quieter, and faster computer was up and running! The transition
freed up hours of work time that could be spent doing projects that had
been deferred because of the battle to keep the old computer system
running.

Encouragement goes a long way for all of us. For a church
secretary a word of encouragement, the gift of a day off, or a card signed
by the office group after the completion of a major project or report can
make the difference between staying or looking for another position with
more pay, better benefits, and less people to deal with. So the best
scenario includes the secretary as a full partner and team member in the
mission and work of the congregation.

TIME AND PLACE

Time and place go together in church life. Time has different meanings in different settings and different church cultures. It is important to consider and understand how time is viewed by the congregation and the community. Place is where the physical assets of the congregation reside, but it is also the location of worship, learning, social interactions, and meetings between people in the congregation. In this section we will explore these concepts and how they intersect and affect each other.

I have a friend that often remarks about the difference between "real time" and "church time." You might be thinking we all have 24 hour days and 168 hours in 7 days per week and that is true. However, real time is the rhythm of life and work generally away from the place labeled church. Church time is identified by the conscious awareness of something happening at church or scheduled to happen at church within the context of the rest of life. So church time is often that period on Sunday mornings when people are at church and focusing on church stuff: information to be shared, programs coming up, and the lesson for children's Sunday School, or the agenda items for the next board meeting. Consequently church time is much smaller in quantity and even quality than real time. Church administrators should contemplate the attention being placed on the schedules, facilities, and events of the church when one is working at the church and for the church versus the awareness of these very same things when one is a regular attender of the church. Church time is when people are consciously present and thinking about church matters.

I've participated in meetings when church leaders volunteered to take on retreat planning or the repair of a hole in the wall in the youth room. The commitments were made on "church time" so as soon as the person moved into "real time" the church related items fell to the bottom or fell off of the priority list. Consequently when church administrators or church staff assumed progress was being made on the projects nothing happened because the entry into "church time" only happened once per week. This can lead to disappointment in the volunteers and a questioning of their loyalty to the church. So the skill of understanding and moving between the two types of time is a wonderful attribute in church administration.

Place is a key concept in church administration. At one time in my journey of church life I believed that the concept of place was relative. In other words a Sunday School class or small group could meet in various rooms or at a coffee shop and could rotate through places without much effect. But my thinking changed when I realized that people sit in the same spot during church services and can get surly if asked to move. On a visit to Hawaii our family attended a church service in a state park along the beach. It was an idyllic setting, but required effort to set up and take down chairs and sound equipment. On the morning we were guests, the pastor was excited to announce the good news that the group would be moving into a "permanent" building in town within the next few weeks.

After 18 years he and the set up team could spend time doing something else!

Place really matters in just about everything related to church life. Even the church staff will settle into a routine of place where they work, how they enter and exit the church building, and the rooms and spaces they use or walk through on a weekly basis. Some readers might chuckle and think that the pastor or church staff can work anywhere as long as they have a computer and a phone. This is true, but even the "virtual" work spaces tend to be at the same coffee shop or the same library, or the same restaurant. We are very place oriented and church administration requires attention to this matter.

It was a Tuesday midmorning at the church. Two women's Bible study groups were scheduled to meet at the same time but in different rooms. Five minutes before the scheduled start time an angry leader came into the church office and said, "They are in our room and we can't meet anywhere else." I listened carefully and tried to remember the room arrangements for these two groups. After checking the church calendar I offered that the meeting rooms had been changed due to some remodeling taking place at the church. "But we've always met in that room and at this time. Why doesn't the other group find a different room?" Mediation between the two groups was required and at last we found appropriate places for both to conduct a Bible study. Times like this may not be the best setting for your mini sermon about servanthood or "in honor preferring one another."

Churches form partnerships with schools, day care programs, music groups needing rehearsal and performance space, and a host of other great groups. Take some time to work out an agreement in writing so that there is a reasonable understanding of the use of the church space by each group at a specific time. A church I worked in entered into a long term space usage agreement with a private school. The agreement for space usage was executed long before I arrived as the church administrator. In my desire to understand the group I began observing and learning about daily and weekly space usage. The school stated in the beginning that it had outgrown a residential basement with a few students and wanted to use the children's educational rooms at the church during the week. After all, little or nothing was happening in these rooms during the week. School leaders stated that the school would be portable: each week teachers would bring in equipment and materials needed for the school and at the end of the week the materials would be loaded back in the vehicles of the school leaders. By the time I arrived on the scene the proverbial elephant was entirely in the tent. Church children's educational rooms had been transformed into school classrooms with sets of reference books, standard student desks and chairs, and computer stations. Church volunteers charged with teaching the church Sunday school programs began to see notes and instructions in the rooms. "Please don't erase the white board." "We've left the lower quarter of the bulletin board for you." "The computer workstations are not to be used by people outside of our school." Clearly the school in its zeal to expand and improve had taken over the space and was less and less willing to share it with church staff and programs. Well the day came when church programming grew and the school also wanted to expand into additional space. Conflicts mounted as school teachers would come to work in "their" rooms during times when the church programs were taking place. Church staff directing children's and youth programs ran into space limitations and had difficulty explaining to volunteer teachers and church families why much of the space was "off limits." Eventually the church leaders asked the school (which wasn't operated by the church) to find a new home where it could expand and enjoy the exclusive use of its own place. There was discord and disruption over this decision, but the church staff and programs were empowered to take possession of space to use in fidelity with the mission of the church. In conclusion let me reiterate the strong sense of place and ownership of particular spaces within a church. Moving individuals and groups around in your church may be more difficult than you think.

TOOLS AND EQUIPMENT

The facility and equipment of a church influence the actions of a congregation and can be a help or a distraction. Church administrators have important work to do in this area. So asking a few questions might help here.

- What was the vision for the property and buildings in the past?
- How is the church using the property, buildings, and equipment to accomplish our current mission?
- What framework is in place to look into the future at tools and equipment for the church?

Learning about the vision for the property and buildings in the past is possible through a look at historical records and conversations with people with the longest relationship with the church. The historical records might include collections of annual reports, milestone celebration booklets for 25 years, 50 years, and more. Often this collection of materials is in the church library or a designated storage area. Looking for a few highlights of building construction, key investments in music instruments, the acquisition of a bus or van, or drives to equip the kitchen should not take a long time. The point is to get a sense of the "what" and the "value" placed on the items described.

There is much to be learned from conversations with people in the congregation about tools and equipment. A good strategy is to ask a person in an informal setting to describe what the congregation was doing when ... Just listen to what they offer and compare the information to what is available in written records. Often the conversation will bring together missing pieces of the story of the tools and equipment of the past.

In one church the lower level was divided into a kitchen and fellowship hall on one end and children's classrooms and a teen area on the other end. Bathrooms were near the kitchen and fellowship hall. Traffic flow from the main level to the fellowship hall seemed difficult and the orientation of the children's and teen areas was odd because the children's rooms were further away from the bathrooms. In a casual conversation one day I was remarking about the distance to the bathrooms for the children in the younger groups. The leader I was talking with offered that when the building was constructed there was a major conversation about which end of the building to put classrooms in and which end of the building to put the fellowship hall in. A change was made and the spaces where traded from what had been planned. So now I knew why there was certain awkwardness about the traffic flow in the lower level of the church building.

During the time I've worked at churches the concept of projected videos and images has become common place. But that was not always the case and it is interesting to think of the changes made in sanctuaries and meeting rooms to accommodate this technology. One church had a large cross prominently mounted in the center of the wall behind the platform. When the time came to have a large screen and a permanently mounted projector, a plan was developed to move the large cross to the side wall. The cross would still be in a very prominent place, but now to the side to make way for the projection area. Well this caused quite a stir among some folks in the congregation. "The cross is central and should stay where it is!" Then the question was posed, "What if we could increase the meaning of our worship and learning time together by making this adjustment?" The logic of using a tool for maximum effectiveness was accepted and the cross was moved and the video projection area remodeled. A new member or a guest would never notice a change had been made. So know how tools and equipment will enhance the experiences of the congregation and serve the mission.

The incorporation of the internet into the operation of churches is common place today. My years of work involved the significant journey of transformation with access to the internet. In the early years we used file boxes of physical clip art. Then we rejoiced when clip art was available on cd's. Now church offices would be hard pressed to work without internet connections to collections of images, video clips, and cloud based tools. On several occasions I've witnessed the exodus of all staff when the internet was down. My youth pastor colleagues were usually the first to say, "I might as well go home, the internet is down." So connections to the internet are expected and useful in church operations.

Not long ago I was in my office at church and noticed a man running cable to a nearby utility pole. This was at the property line of the church and I was curious enough to engage him in conversation. He offered that his company was installing high speed internet to the entire neighborhood around the church. I asked, "Does this mean the church would have access to high speed internet too?" Getting 10 times the speed and capacity of internet service at double the cost of current operations seemed like a good idea to me. Fortunately the church leadership agreed and today the congregation is stepping into digital services for uploading and downloading content that were literally impossible and unaffordable a short time ago. The congregation will benefit from decisions that enlarge the tools for learning and for sharing the core message of the church. Be vigilant about leveraging the tools of technology to bless the congregation and the community around the church.

I've often remarked that paint and new flooring are relatively inexpensive, but entirely new structures and extensive remodeling are costly. Over the years I've observed churches as they built structures: some were obviously to be left permanently in a particular configuration and some were designed to accommodate change. I've met an architect with the theory that churches should build for today's needs, but provide for changes in the future. One sanctuary was designed so that a wall could be easily taken out and the building extended. Another building was constructed with a doorway that could easily be opened through a wall. Working in church administration you can set the congregation up for success well into the future by making allowances for new structures and tools that will be of tremendous benefit.

A Word About Congregational DNA

Church organizations have culture and personality. Ask yourself, "What is the DNA of my church?" Included in this topic is a basketful of things: why the church was started, when the church was started, the identity and mission of the founders, shaping events, personality and legacy of pastors and key leaders, and more! It is helpful to understand and describe the DNA of a church if you are going to succeed and if you purpose to make changes.

Some of you may be thinking, "What difference does it make? Our church is committed to spreading the gospel." Good point, but perception today matters a great deal and current and prospective participants in the congregation will run into the DNA of your church. Many churches were started out of a profound sense of calling and mission. Does that historical framework still speak to those entering your church? Other churches were started because of a "split" or a disagreement so strong that a group left the original congregation to start a new one. Some folks I know describe this as more of a divorce than a friendly parting of the ways. In any case in the administration of a church you will have to deal with and perhaps reshape the DNA of the church were you are working.

One church was started because of the calling and drive of a woman in the 1800's that felt there should be a Sunday school for children and eventually a church in the newly formed frontier community. She rounded up like minded people and began a Sunday School. Within a few years the church called its first pastor and took in a group of charter members. After a few more years the congregation built a building and was the first congregation to have a permanent building in the city. This church has surpassed its 100th birthday and the DNA of outreach, Sunday School for children, and making a difference in the community is alive and well. Over the years attendance has grown and declined, pastors of very different personalities and styles have come and gone, but the core DNA of the congregation is alive and can be felt when the congregation gathers.

Guests notice it and remark about it in positive comments. It is truly what sets this congregation apart from others in the area.

On the other hand is a congregation started from a "split" in the 1950's? If you drive by the building you might wonder if it has changed at all from the era in which it was built. Entering the building for the first time you might get a visual dose of all the things "we are not." The decor speaks to real separation and distance from the current culture. If a conversation starts with a member it might be evident that "We are glad a stranger like you dropped in." When the DNA of a church highlights differences, disparages other nearby churches, and quickly highlights how unique the church is – well it might point to a miserable and slow death for the church. If you are involved in leadership and administration take stock of church DNA and figure out if it is good, if it is changeable, and where you stand.

MY GUESS ABOUT THE FUTURE OF CHURCH

I'll confess that I'm an optimist about the future of church. The legacy of over 2000 years of continuous operation in the middle of great national, cultural, and economic change is cause to celebrate the resiliency of church. I've traveled a fair amount and noticed that people in every culture and on every continent are incurably religious. The number of church buildings scattered around the world is truly amazing and a testament to the commitment of the people of every place to have a dedicated place to worship. So my perspective is that churches will continue to exist long into the future in the midst of lots of change.

Quite a few years ago I was part of a group that wanted to start a new church. The mother church wanted to birth a new church into a successful journey of its own. On a clear sunny afternoon I met with a district church leader with hopes in learning some great insight into starting a new church. After welcoming me into his office he reached into a file drawer in his desk and took out a folder and offered it to me. He said, "Well here are some plans that have been used to construct church buildings." The remainder of the conversation revolved around acquiring property and building a structure for a new congregation. This was the perspective of, "if you build it they will come." I left the meeting that day wondering if that approach was as valid as it may have been at one time.

This is the era of a smorgasbord of ways to start new congregations. My sense is every method has relevance depending on the circumstances. The concept of house churches is alive and well. These are small groups that meet in a home with or without a pastor. The community is intimate and a high level of personal interaction is possible between members. The problem is what to do when the group gets too large for a home. It is possible to divide into another house church, but often folks want to continue to be together and embark on a journey to seek a larger space. Eventually growth leads to an established congregation with property and facilities. The maturing house church takes on the characteristics of other established churches.

Another model is that of a congregation or group of congregations starting a congregation in a new place. Perhaps a large church in the Southeast part of the United States develops a calling to start a new congregation in the Northwest part of the United States. The leaders and resources are assembled and a group comes into a community with a plan and takes steps to establish a church where none existed. This type of activity is normal and occurs on a regular basis. With support and encouragement the congregation takes root and moves along to independence. The success rate is higher because of the flow of support in the formative time of the new congregation.

Individuals have life transforming experiences and may embark on a journey to establish a church in the area where they live. This might begin as a house church, move to rented retail space, and eventually end up with a standalone facility. Administration will develop along the journey as people and circumstances change. Many times the founder will not be the person leading the congregation after it becomes established and things become more complex.

Some congregations share buildings. This is interesting because administration requires someone to be in charge of maintenance, cleaning, repairs, and decision-making with regard to the buildings and property. Usually one group owns the building and property and rents it to other groups.

As a church leader or administrator you may find yourself in one or more of the above scenarios. Each has its advantages and disadvantages, but the future church will continue to creatively inhabit different styles. We live in an era of great choice and I think that will continue.

NOW WHAT?

If you've read this far – congratulations! If you work as a church administrator you are to be commended. If you are in leadership in your local church then my hope is that the content of this book will serve to support your efforts. I challenge you to set aside some time to make your own evaluation of each of the topics covered and see how your own church is functioning. Perhaps there are ways to collaborate with your pastor, church staff, and leaders that will bless your congregation and the community around you. My conviction is that your church is too important to allow it to exist without careful consideration of how to make it more effective!

www.ingramcontent.com/pod-product-compliance
Lightning Source LLC
Chambersburg PA
CBHW051358280526
45784CB00007B/3001